Stop and Ask Yourself

Questions of the Mind

Carissa Black & Zeev Yosef

Stop and Ask Yourself
Copyright © 2021 by Carissa Black and Zeev Yosef
All Rights Reserved

All rights reserved. No part of this publication may be reproduced, distributed, or transmitted in any form or by any means, including photocopying, recording, or other electronic or mechanical methods, without the prior written permission of the AUTHOR, except in the case of brief quotations embodied in critical reviews and certain other noncommercial uses permitted by copyright law.

This book is not intended as a substitute for the medical advice of physicians. The reader should regularly consult a physician in matters relating to his/her health and particularly with respect to any symptoms that may require diagnosis or medical attention.

Publisher: Absolute Author Publishing House
Editor: Dr. Melissa Caudle
Logo Design: Ohr Elcayam

Paperback ISBN: 978-1-64953-209-1

This book is dedicated to the expansion of the good vibe tribe to ultimately make the world a better place.

Carissa Black & Zeev Yosef

HOW TO USE THIS BOOK

Change the way you look at things; everything around you will change. Since we cannot change others or situations, the change should be in us. Raising our vibe can make a world of difference. You might be asking yourself, "How you can raise your vibe?" The answer to your question lies within your thoughts! Positive thinking can propel you forward. It will lead you to take positive action, and like wind beneath your wings, it will take you higher.

They say that positivity is contagious. Your positivity will spread, and touch those around you. The first step in making a positive impact is asking the right questions. Positive thought-provoking questions can raise your vibe frequency, which leads to daily reflection, journaling, tracking habits, and goal setting. Open your mind! Expand your thinking! Raise your vibe and bring about positive change to ultimately know yourself on a deeper level. Use this opportunity to increase your discipline and compound good habits. The questions provided can result in healing, growth, and awareness.

There are many ways this book could be used. Please act as if you were writing it; THIS IS FOR YOU! Not only should you answer the questions that may lead to

STOP AND ASK YOURSELF

journaling, but also think as to why this is a question, how and what shaped your answer, and ask yourself a variation of the question or how someone else might answer it. Engage your mind, remind yourself of things forgotten and think forward. Share the emotions and experiences, listen to others, and keep the good vibes flowing!

There are two parts to this book. The first consists of questions. The more honest you are with yourself, the more growth in yourself. The second part consists of a Call to Action. When you see this symbol below, it means that you are to take action before moving on to the next set of questions.

Enjoy!

Carissa Black and Zeev Yosef

Carissa Black & Zeev Yosef

Q's

What do you find as a high-value item? Why?

_____
_____
_____
_____
_____
_____
_____
_____

What meal can turn your day around? Why?

_____
_____
_____
_____
_____
_____
_____
_____

STOP AND ASK YOURSELF

When do you feel your best? Why?

_____
_____
_____
_____
_____
_____
_____
_____

What might scare you that doesn't scare others? Why?

_____
_____
_____
_____
_____
_____
_____
_____

Do you receive criticism well? Why or why not?

_____
_____
_____
_____
_____
_____
_____
_____

Carissa Black & Zeev Yosef

Do you prefer music with lyrics? Why or why not?

How long does it take you to adapt to new information?

What would cause you to stop speaking with someone?

STOP AND ASK YOURSELF

Reflect on the fallout and see what your part was. Are you ready to repair the relationship? What action can you take to make amends?

_____
_____
_____
_____
_____
_____
_____

Did you accept your part in this? Why or why not?

_____
_____
_____
_____
_____
_____
_____

Carissa Black & Zeev Yosef

What is the oldest object you own?

What could you make from just a pair of scissors?

If you were a business partner, what skills would you provide?

STOP AND ASK YOURSELF

List what businesses use these skills.

1. _____
2. _____
3. _____
4. _____
5. _____
6. _____
7. _____
8. _____
9. _____
10. _____

List businesses that you can create using these skills.

1. _____
2. _____
3. _____
4. _____
5. _____
6. _____
7. _____
8. _____
9. _____
10. _____

Carissa Black & Zeev Yosef

What would be or has been your favorite live performance? Why?

List ways to outsource paying rent.

What is your biggest expense?

STOP AND ASK YOURSELF

Write down everything you spend money on immediately for a week. After, label each expense need or want.

DATE	EXPENSE	NEED OR WANT

Carissa Black & Zeev Yosef

Review your expenses from last week? What spending patterns can you identify?

_____
_____
_____
_____
_____
_____
_____

Is there room for improvement? Why or why not?

_____
_____
_____
_____
_____
_____
_____

What steps can you take to make a difference in your spending habits?

_____
_____
_____
_____
_____
_____
_____
_____

STOP AND ASK YOURSELF

Have you made a plan for saving for the future or for an emergency expense? Why or why not?

_____
_____
_____
_____
_____
_____
_____

What figurative seeds do you plant in conversation?

_____
_____
_____
_____
_____
_____
_____

What is your elevator pitch?

_____
_____
_____
_____
_____
_____
_____
_____

Share your pitch with at least four people and listen to their reactions. Use the form below to identify them for the pitch and write down their response.

PERSON	WRITE DOWN THEIR RESPONSE

STOP AND ASK YOURSELF

What values do you hold dearest? Why?

_____
_____
_____
_____
_____
_____
_____

What movie would you live in? Why?

_____
_____
_____
_____
_____
_____
_____

Why do you think people admire you? Or, if they don't, why?

_____
_____
_____
_____
_____
_____
_____

Carissa Black & Zeev Yosef

Describe good service:

What did you despise growing up but love now? What changed?

What is it about someone that really grinds your gears?

STOP AND ASK YOURSELF

If you are easily angered, what can you do to control your temper?

___

When was the last time you became mad at someone? What was the outcome?

___

What is a limiting belief you can overcome?

___

Carissa Black & Zeev Yosef

List any limiting beliefs, how were they imposed? Write actions you'll take to remove these limits in the table below.

LIMITING BELIEF	HOW IMPOSED	ACTIONS

STOP AND ASK YOURSELF

What makes an experience meaningful?

_____
_____
_____
_____
_____
_____

What value did your most recent hundred-dollar or more purchase provide?

_____
_____
_____
_____
_____
_____
_____

What is the difference between stingy and frugal?

_____
_____
_____
_____
_____
_____
_____
_____

Carissa Black & Zeev Yosef

What song can change your mood? Why does it work?

What would you choose, convenience or comfort? Why?

Do you track your performance? Why or why not?

STOP AND ASK YOURSELF

Make a daily and weekly habit tracker.

SUN	MON	TUES	WED	THURS	FRI	SAT

List one habit you have in the following categories.

Health: _____

Family: _____

Social: _____

Work Related: _____

Financial: _____

Asses at the end of the week and continue to grow more healthy habits while keeping the consistency.

Carissa Black & Zeev Yosef

What positive things would people say at your funeral?

_____
_____
_____
_____
_____
_____

What lifestyle do you promote? How and why?

_____
_____
_____
_____
_____
_____
_____
_____
_____
_____

If you were to move cities what would you miss the most?

_____
_____
_____
_____
_____
_____
_____
_____
_____

STOP AND ASK YOURSELF

What do you think makes you more of a man or woman? Why?

_____
_____
_____
_____
_____
_____

What is something you dislike that people do to you but might be doing to other people?

_____
_____
_____
_____
_____
_____
_____
_____
_____
_____

What do you consider a high value skill?

_____
_____
_____
_____
_____
_____
_____
_____

Carissa Black & Zeev Yosef

If you lived close to the beach how would your life change?

If you had a choice, would you rather live in the mountains or in a city? Why?

What is something you wish you learned earlier?

STOP AND ASK YOURSELF

List, DIY projects, applications or books you want to read and get involved in. Commit 20 minutes to learning daily.

DIY PROJECTS

1. _____
2. _____
3. _____
4. _____
5. _____

BOOKS TO READ

1. _____
2. _____
3. _____
4. _____
5. _____

APPLICATIONS TO LEARN

1. _____
2. _____
3. _____
4. _____
5. _____

Carissa Black & Zeev Yosef

List businesses that you can create using the skills, experience, or knowledge learned from DYI project, books, or applications.

1. _____
2. _____
3. _____
4. _____
5. _____

Does one ring truer for you? Why or why not?

_____
_____
_____
_____
_____
_____

What is something you wish you understood better?

_____
_____
_____
_____
_____
_____
_____
_____
_____
_____
_____
_____

STOP AND ASK YOURSELF

What practices can you implement to become more of a go-getter?

_____
_____
_____
_____
_____
_____

How do you raise the average of the five people you hang out with?

_____
_____
_____
_____
_____

What makes your birthday meaningful?

_____
_____
_____
_____
_____
_____
_____
_____
_____

Carissa Black & Zeev Yosef

List five keys to success?

1. _____
2. _____
3. _____
4. _____
5. _____

In what ways do you take control?

_____
_____
_____
_____
_____
_____

List goals that are preposterous.

1. _____
2. _____
3. _____
4. _____
5. _____

Give an example when you last paid it forward?

_____
_____
_____
_____
_____
_____

STOP AND ASK YOURSELF

Find time this week to pay it forward, no matter how small the act is. Be creative by taking action, donate your time, money, or advice. Brainstorm your ideas and record your pay it forward actions in the following section below.

PERSON TO PAY IT FORWARD	HOW WILL YOU PAY IT FORWARD	SET A DATE TO PAY IT FORWARD	WHAT WAS THE PERSON'S RESPONSE?

Carissa Black & Zeev Yosef

What did you learn from paying it forward?
_____
_____
_____
_____
_____

What values were instilled in you as a child?
_____
_____
_____
_____
_____

What are you looking for in a work of art?
_____
_____
_____
_____
_____

List what you're grateful for.
_____
_____
_____
_____
_____

STOP AND ASK YOURSELF

Challenge yourself to write daily lists, before you go to sleep and as you wake. Here is a To-Do lists for the next seven days. Get in the habit of writing them down at the end of the day, so you can complete them the next day. Be sure to check them off as you complete each task.

TO-DO LIST   DATE: _____

- ○ _____
- ○ _____
- ○ _____
- ○ _____
- ○ _____
- ○ _____
- ○ _____
- ○ _____
- ○ _____
- ○ _____
- ○ _____
- ○ _____
- ○ _____
- ○ _____
- ○ _____
- ○ _____
- ○ _____
- ○ _____

Carissa Black & Zeev Yosef

TO-DO LIST   DATE: _____

- ○ _____
- ○ _____
- ○ _____
- ○ _____
- ○ _____
- ○ _____
- ○ _____
- ○ _____
- ○ _____
- ○ _____
- ○ _____
- ○ _____
- ○ _____

TO-DO LIST   DATE: _____

- ○ _____
- ○ _____
- ○ _____
- ○ _____
- ○ _____
- ○ _____
- ○ _____
- ○ _____
- ○ _____
- ○ _____
- ○ _____
- ○ _____
- ○ _____

STOP AND ASK YOURSELF

TO-DO LIST   DATE: _____

- _____
- _____
- _____
- _____
- _____
- _____
- _____
- _____
- _____
- _____
- _____
- _____
- _____

TO-DO LIST   DATE: _____

- _____
- _____
- _____
- _____
- _____
- _____
- _____
- _____
- _____
- _____
- _____
- _____
- _____

Carissa Black & Zeev Yosef

TO-DO LIST   DATE: _____

- ☐ _____
- ☐ _____
- ☐ _____
- ☐ _____
- ☐ _____
- ☐ _____
- ☐ _____
- ☐ _____
- ☐ _____
- ☐ _____
- ☐ _____
- ☐ _____
- ☐ _____

TO-DO LIST   DATE: _____

- ☐ _____
- ☐ _____
- ☐ _____
- ☐ _____
- ☐ _____
- ☐ _____
- ☐ _____
- ☐ _____
- ☐ _____
- ☐ _____
- ☐ _____
- ☐ _____
- ☐ _____

STOP AND ASK YOURSELF

How do you bounce back from failure?

_____
_____
_____
_____
_____

Write a memory that brings you joy.

_____
_____
_____
_____
_____

What would make you trust a stranger?

_____
_____
_____
_____
_____

What advice would you give to someone who has lost everything?

_____
_____
_____
_____
_____

Carissa Black & Zeev Yosef

What is a sensitive subject for you? Why?

How do you like to communicate?

What countries would be on the list for your world tour?

What qualities would you want your children to have?

STOP AND ASK YOURSELF

List fun facts.

1. _____
2. _____
3. _____
4. _____
5. _____
6. _____
7. _____
8. _____
9. _____
10. _____

Which meal is most important to you? Why?

_____
_____
_____
_____
_____

Describe your favorite social gathering.

_____
_____
_____
_____
_____
_____
_____
_____
_____
_____
_____

Carissa Black & Zeev Yosef

What do you consider romantic?

_____
_____
_____
_____
_____

What opportunity would you wait in line for?

_____
_____
_____
_____
_____

Define home.

_____
_____
_____
_____
_____

How can you be more sustainable?

_____
_____
_____
_____
_____
_____
_____
_____

STOP AND ASK YOURSELF

List ways you can make, or reuse items frequently used. Grow your own food, make your own tooth paste, or

1. _____
2. _____
3. _____
4. _____
5. _____
6. _____
7. _____
8. _____
9. _____
10. _____

Would you be interested in actually doing these things? Why or why not?

_____
_____
_____
_____
_____
_____
_____
_____
_____
_____

Carissa Black & Zeev Yosef

How important is being punctual? Why?

How do you want others to interpret when you "give your word"?

Describe a humorous miscommunication you've had with another person.

What are the morals of your stories?

STOP AND ASK YOURSELF

What smells do you like? Why?

_____
_____
_____
_____

List things that are weird and cool.

1. _____
2. _____
3. _____
4. _____
5. _____
6. _____
7. _____
8. _____
9. _____
10. _____

What would your *Ted Talk* topic be? Why?

_____
_____
_____
_____
_____
_____
_____
_____
_____
_____
_____
_____

Carissa Black & Zeev Yosef

Write your presentation script. Share your written lecture aloud.

STOP AND ASK YOURSELF

What do you wish for the most? Why?

_____
_____
_____
_____
_____
_____
_____

What things in your life would you like to change?

_____
_____
_____
_____
_____
_____
_____
_____
_____
_____
_____
_____
_____
_____
_____

Carissa Black & Zeev Yosef

Meditate, journal, or create a vision board. Think about this wish and how you could manifest it. What steps could you take to make that wish would come true?

Write 10 positive affirmations to tell yourself daily.

1. _____
2. _____
3. _____
4. _____
5. _____
6. _____
7. _____
8. _____
9. _____
10. _____

Now choose one or two of the affirmations from above and write them on a sticky note. Place the sticky notes on your mirror and read them every day.

Share one positive affirmation with one other person.

Who: _____ _____ Completed

STOP AND ASK YOURSELF

What is your favorite means of travel without and engine? Why?

_____
_____
_____
_____
_____
_____
_____
_____

Recall a "close call."

_____
_____
_____
_____
_____
_____
_____
_____

Describe a headline you wish to see in the news.

_____
_____
_____
_____
_____
_____
_____
_____

Carissa Black & Zeev Yosef

From where would you send a post-card? Why? And, who would you send to it.

What would your post-card say?

Describe your idea of a donation.

STOP AND ASK YOURSELF

Describe a positive obsession.

_____
_____
_____
_____
_____

List things you can build.

1. _____
2. _____
3. _____
4. _____
5. _____

What makes you original? Why?

_____
_____
_____
_____

What do you own that no longer serves you a purpose?

_____
_____
_____
_____
_____
_____

Carissa Black & Zeev Yosef

What do you enjoy to do when it's cold? Why?

_____
_____
_____
_____
_____
_____
_____
_____

What activities do you think of when it's summer?

_____
_____
_____
_____
_____
_____
_____
_____

What's more important; the journey or destination? Why?

_____
_____
_____
_____
_____
_____
_____
_____

STOP AND ASK YOURSELF

What are, in your eyes, the wonders of the world? Why?

_____
_____
_____
_____
_____
_____
_____
_____

Are you easy to love? Why or why not?

_____
_____
_____
_____
_____
_____
_____
_____

Where would fly over in a hot air balloon? Why?

_____
_____
_____
_____
_____
_____
_____
_____

Carissa Black & Zeev Yosef

Is it difficult to identify the positive inside the negative? Why or why not?

Is it fuel or failure?

How do you view yourself?

STOP AND ASK YOURSELF

List ways you can turn failures into fuel.

1. _____
2. _____
3. _____
4. _____
5. _____

Write down the barriers you face?

_____
_____
_____
_____
_____
_____
_____
_____

Make a plan to overcome these barriers.

_____
_____
_____

Carissa Black & Zeev Yosef

How do you celebrate success?

_____
_____
_____
_____
_____
_____
_____
_____

List the qualities of a good host.

1. _____
2. _____
3. _____
4. _____
5. _____

If you were given the opportunity to be a good host, how would you act?

_____
_____
_____
_____
_____
_____
_____
_____

STOP AND ASK YOURSELF

Arrange a get-together for your friends or family. Be creative and detail-oriented by using this table as a planning guide.

Name of Guests	What Theme?	How will you invite them?	What will you serve?	What drinks will you provide?

Carissa Black & Zeev Yosef

What do you tell yourself when things don't go as expected?

What would you grow on your farm?

How can you start?

STOP AND ASK YOURSELF

What helps you make a difficult choice?

_____
_____
_____
_____
_____
_____
_____
_____

Do you believe things happen for you or happen to you? Why or why not?

_____
_____
_____
_____
_____
_____
_____
_____

Is being noticed important to you? Why or why not?

_____
_____
_____
_____
_____
_____
_____
_____

Carissa Black & Zeev Yosef

Describe how you would like to be recognized?

___

Who do you mimic? Why?

___

What do you classify as heroic?

___

STOP AND ASK YOURSELF

Who would you host in your guest bedroom?

_____
_____
_____
_____
_____
_____
_____

What are your uplifting go to mottos? List as many as you can.

_____
_____
_____
_____
_____
_____
_____
_____
_____
_____
_____
_____
_____
_____
_____
_____
_____
_____

Carissa Black & Zeev Yosef

Who has given you the best advice? What was it?

What advice would you give to another adult?

What advice would you give to a teen or a child?

STOP AND ASK YOURSELF

Thank a person for their advice. List ways of sharing this advice and who it would benefit?

_____
_____
_____
_____
_____
_____
_____
_____

If you could share a message with the world what would it be?

_____
_____
_____
_____
_____
_____
_____
_____

Carissa Black & Zeev Yosef

Why? What is the intention?

_____
_____
_____
_____
_____
_____
_____
_____

How do you celebrate your birthday? Why?

_____
_____
_____
_____
_____
_____
_____
_____

What do you enjoy indulging in? Why?

_____
_____
_____
_____
_____
_____
_____
_____
_____

STOP AND ASK YOURSELF

What is your human design? Go online to jovianarchive.com to find out.

_____
_____
_____
_____
_____
_____
_____
_____

Review your blueprint find any confluence with how you make decisions and live your true self.

_____
_____
_____
_____
_____
_____
_____
_____

If you could take a whole year off, what would you?

_____
_____
_____
_____
_____
_____
_____
_____

Carissa Black & Zeev Yosef

What's stopping you? How can you work through them?

What causes are important to you? Why?

What was your first job? What did you learn from it?

STOP AND ASK YOURSELF

What have you learned that has greatly changed your perspective? How did it change?

_____
_____
_____
_____
_____
_____
_____

What information do you like to share with people?

_____
_____
_____
_____
_____
_____
_____

How can it be more positive?

_____
_____
_____
_____
_____
_____
_____
_____

Carissa Black & Zeev Yosef

Do you easily forgive? Why?

How do you define recreation and hobbies?

What are yours?

STOP AND ASK YOURSELF

How many times in your life have you moved?

Where was your favorite place you lived?

If you could live in any era what would it be? Why?

Carissa Black & Zeev Yosef

Who was your favorite teacher? Why?

What is something new you're learning?

What value does it bring?

STOP AND ASK YOURSELF

Describe the best version of yourself.

_____
_____
_____
_____
_____
_____
_____
_____

Who has impacted your life the most? How and why?

_____
_____
_____
_____
_____
_____
_____
_____

What do you care about? Why?

_____
_____
_____
_____
_____
_____
_____
_____

Carissa Black & Zeev Yosef

Do you like traveling?

_____
_____
_____
_____
_____
_____
_____

What do you like about it

_____
_____
_____
_____
_____
_____
_____

What was your favorite childhood memory? Why?

_____
_____
_____
_____
_____
_____
_____

STOP AND ASK YOURSELF

Are you interested in history? Why or why not?

_____
_____
_____
_____
_____
_____
_____
_____

Do you have a hard time saying no? Why or why not?

_____
_____
_____
_____
_____
_____
_____
_____

List what motivates you.

_____
_____
_____
_____
_____
_____
_____
_____

Carissa Black & Zeev Yosef

Do you take risks? Why or why not?

_____
_____
_____
_____
_____
_____
_____
_____

Do you do volunteer work? Why or why not?

_____
_____
_____
_____
_____
_____
_____
_____

Is being of service to others important to you? Why or why not?

_____
_____
_____
_____
_____
_____
_____
_____

STOP AND ASK YOURSELF

How can you live a healthier lifestyle?

Are you accountable?

How could you be better?

Carissa Black & Zeev Yosef

In what do you invest? Why?

_____
_____
_____
_____
_____
_____
_____
_____

What moments in your life have brought about change? How were those changes positive?

_____
_____
_____
_____
_____
_____
_____
_____

What does love mean to you? Why?

_____
_____
_____
_____
_____
_____
_____
_____

STOP AND ASK YOURSELF

Does being an entrepreneur interest you? Why or why not?

_____
_____
_____
_____
_____
_____
_____
_____

Do you make time in your week for self-care? Why or why not?

_____
_____
_____
_____
_____
_____
_____
_____

List qualities do you seek in friends and partners.

_____
_____
_____
_____
_____
_____
_____
_____

Carissa Black & Zeev Yosef

As a child what was your favorite toy or playtime activity? Why?

_____
_____
_____
_____
_____
_____
_____
_____

If a stranger met you, what positive things do you think they would say?

_____
_____
_____
_____
_____
_____
_____
_____

What is your perfect day? Why?

_____
_____
_____
_____
_____
_____
_____
_____

STOP AND ASK YOURSELF

Schedule a date to recreate your perfect day. Follow through with as many actions as possible.

Describe how your perfect date went.

_____
_____
_____
_____
_____
_____
_____
_____
_____
_____
_____
_____
_____
_____
_____
_____
_____
_____

Carissa Black & Zeev Yosef

What brings you inspiration? Why?

Do you listen to your gut? Why?

What lessons have come from it?

STOP AND ASK YOURSELF

What is your favorite holiday or celebration? Why?

_____
_____
_____
_____
_____
_____
_____
_____

What is your go to outfit? Why?

_____
_____
_____
_____
_____
_____
_____
_____

What cultures do you identify or relate with? Why?

_____
_____
_____
_____
_____
_____
_____
_____
_____
_____

Carissa Black & Zeev Yosef

If you could be a twin, would you? Why?

_____
_____
_____
_____
_____
_____
_____
_____

Do you rely on something to help start your day? Why or why not?

_____
_____
_____
_____
_____
_____
_____
_____

How do you like to end your days? Why?

_____
_____
_____
_____
_____
_____
_____
_____

STOP AND ASK YOURSELF

What work could be done to improve your thought process?

_____
_____
_____
_____
_____
_____
_____
_____

What movie, as a child, inspired you? Why?

_____
_____
_____
_____
_____
_____
_____
_____

What does grounding mean to you?

_____
_____
_____
_____
_____
_____
_____
_____
_____
_____

Carissa Black & Zeev Yosef

What do you do to ground yourself?

What does getting married mean to you?

Do you believe in astrology or have an interest in it? Why or why not?

STOP AND ASK YOURSELF

Map your rising, moon, and sun sign. What house do they lie and w hat does it mean? Search for any confluence. Go online to find out by visiting Caféastrology.com.

Rising Sign: _____
Moon Sign: _____
Sun Sign: _____

Do you think everyone is here to fulfill a purpose?

_____
_____
_____
_____
_____
_____
_____
_____

Why or why not?

_____
_____
_____
_____
_____
_____
_____

Carissa Black & Zeev Yosef

What signs have told you that you're on your path?

Do you know yourself well? How do you know?

What things do you like to do alone?

STOP AND ASK YOURSELF

Do you enjoy them more alone? Why?

_____
_____
_____
_____
_____
_____
_____
_____

What did you learn about yourself last year?

_____
_____
_____
_____
_____
_____
_____
_____

What more can you offer the world?

_____
_____
_____
_____
_____
_____
_____
_____

Carissa Black & Zeev Yosef

Have you ever felt drawn to a city or country? Which One? Why do you think that is?

What makes you nervous? Why?

In what ways have you grown in the last year?

STOP AND ASK YOURSELF

How do you connect to people?

___

How could creating checklist help you?

___

What are the five love languages?

___

Carissa Black & Zeev Yosef

Which do you resonate with?
___
___
___
___
___
___
___
___
___

STOP AND ASK YOURSELF

Everyday questions you forget to ask yourself to keep the positive vibes flowing. Exercise your positive vibes muscle! A question a day keeps the bad vibes away. Come join the good vibe tribe and ask yourself questions that promote positive thinking and expansion of the mind.

www.ingramcontent.com/pod-product-compliance
Lightning Source LLC
LaVergne TN
LVHW051151080426
835508LV00021B/2581